To Andy + Jo

THE MAGIC OF MIKINDANI
IMAGES FROM THE SWAHILI COAST

Best Wishes

First published in Great Britain in 2008
by Trade Aid, 11 Glasshouse Studios, Fryern Court Road, Burgate, Fordingbridge, Hampshire, SP6 1QX

Text and photographs©Lawrence Coleman, 2008

All rights reserved. Without limiting the right under copy
reserved above, no part of this publication may be reproduced,
stored or introduced into a retrieval system or transmitted, in
any form or by any means (electronic, mechanical, photocopying,
recording or otherwise) without the prior written permission of
the copyright holder and publisher.

ISBN 978-0-9560532-0-6

Book designed by Sofia Cababie
Artwork prepared at Trade Aid

Production: Lawrence Coleman, Makonde Photography (www.makondephotography.com)
Printing & Binding: KAI LAM DESIGN & PRINTING CO. Rm 1114,
Hong Man Industrial Centre, 2 Hong Man Street, Chi Wan, Hong Kong

Dedicated to Ali Mapolulu

INTRODUCTION

This book is the result of a photographic journey experienced whilst living for more than three years in the town of Mikindani in Southern Tanzania. I first went there as a gap-year student almost a decade ago and have returned more than twenty times, each visit adding to my precious memories. It is neither a large town, nor an internationally famous one, but it has a unique character which draws me back again and again.

Today, Mikindani is a placid backwater, a small town on the coastline of one of Tanzania's poorest regions. It is blessed with a peerless location on the edge of a heart-shaped bay, which forms an ideal natural harbour and protects it from the unpredictable waters of the Indian Ocean. The bay itself is a calm, blue expanse, fringed with coconut palms and shielded by twin peninsula that are thickly covered with mangroves and ancient baobab trees. Enclosed by three hills, the periphery of the town has been dappled more recently by the construction of numerous wattle and daub mud huts. Standing on one of the hills you can hear sounds which are familiar to any African village: children's voices calling to one another, birds singing, crickets chirruping and frogs croaking. The landscape is never silent. Five times a day the Imam calls the Muslim population to prayer. Old men in skullcaps and robes shuffle down the streets to the mosque, their sandals kicking up dust along the sandy paths.

Every morning at sunrise majestic dhows spread their sails against the amber sky and dugout canoes return from night fishing with their catch. Life almost comes to a standstill under the hot afternoon sun as colour is bleached from the landscape and the sky assumes a fierce ultramarine blue. When evening falls, a haze of smoke appears among the treetops of the coconut palms as each household starts a fire in preparation for the evening meal. These are sights and sounds that can be experienced in Tanzania, Angola, the Gambia or almost anywhere in coastal Africa. What makes Mikindani unique is the setting in which these daily events unfold.

Upon closer inspection, the town reveals a patchwork of cultural influences; a German fort, a Hindu temple, an old slave market, Shia and Sunni mosques and Evangelical and Catholic churches. Grand two-storey buildings populate the old town, their limewash coating fallen away to reveal large blocks of coral rag underneath. Few places can boast such an array of influences or the same degree of cultural infusion. It is amid this historical tapestry that today people go about their daily lives, however, it is impossible to separate the place from its past.

Undeniably, it is the people of Mikindani that have drawn me back time and again. They have always shown an interest in me as a visitor and, in the early days, had the patience to traverse the language barrier between us. As in any developing society, the community of Mikindani comprises mainly children. At first, a few were terrified by the sight of me, some were inquisitive, others were daring enough to run right up to me and then flee. It was the children who lived close to my home who gave me my first lessons in Swahili, the national language, and Makonde, the main tribal language of the region. I learned by mimicking their phrases, words and pronunciation. As a result, my Swahili is fluent but laden with street slang and somewhat comical compared with the textbook Swahili taught in the classrooms of foreign language schools.

My first six months in Mikindani were a time of perpetual culture shock; everything seemed exotic to my senses. I began to practice photography, I think, to capture the fleeting moments and vivid experiences that were shaping my life there and preserve them as memories. At the time, I had a small, plastic, compact camera worth no more than thirty pounds. However, I grew frustrated by the fact that my pictures did not show the landscapes, environment and events of daily life in East Africa as they appeared to me.

After a year, I took the plunge and purchased a new camera worth almost my entire monthly salary. The difference was incredible. My pictures were sharper, clearer, more punchy and dynamic. I started to take more and more photographs and carried the camera with me everywhere, much to the amusement of my colleagues! By concentrating on learning from my mistakes, I gradually improved. I slowed down and became more selective about the subject matter. I started to consider composition, exposure and the quality and direction of the light before pressing the shutter release. The process gradually moved from taking snaps to creating photographs.

As I learned and developed my skills, I began to experiment with different films and techniques in an attempt to develop my own approach. At first I sought to capture the deep hues and saturated colours of the landscape; the azure of the Indian Ocean, the silvers and blues of sunrise over the bay and the warm, glowing reds and oranges of the African sunsets. After some time, I began to experiment with monochrome and infrared films, to capture the contrasts, textures and subtle tones that were all around me. Consequently this book is divided into two sections to reflect two distinct styles, colour and monochrome. Although the two sections have distinct styles and subtly different subject matter, I feel they are complementary, and together they present different aspects of my experiences in Tanzania.

I am proud of the fact that none of my images are contrived. I don't instruct people where to stand or what to do and never pay people to take their photograph. I simply try to capture what I see in order to reflect the reality of life in Mikindani. Many of the men and women in these pictures are my good friends and neighbours and each time I return, I distribute prints from my previous trip. By doing so, many of my friends now have their first pictures of themselves, their children and their belongings. The trust and mutual benefit that this brings has allowed me to capture the more poignant and intimate moments in their lives.

It has been a privilege to photograph the people and the town of Mikindani and to build up a collage of life there. I am pleased that the proceeds from this book will go to the charity Trade Aid and will fund projects that work to alleviate poverty in this community. Above all, I hope that the images in the book will provide you with an insight into the culture and environment of Mikindani and will reveal, if just a little, of what makes it such a unique place.

I hope that you enjoy the book.

Lawrence Coleman
Mikindani, Tanzania, August 2008

MIKINDANI IN COLOUR

THE HISTORY OF MIKINDANI

Mikindani is one of the most distinctive towns on the Swahili Coast, which runs from Kenya, along Tanzania and down to Mozambique following the continental shelf of East Africa. Exposure to the Indian Ocean and relative proximity to both the Arabian Peninsula and Indian subcontinent have shaped the history of the coastline and the culture of the societies that live there.

Along with Kilwa and Stone Town in Zanzibar, Mikindani is part of a triumvirate of unique, historic towns which display a cultural infusion; it is possible to see church spires, Hindu temples, mosque minarets and colonial forts all within a short walk of one another.

It is likely that the first settlement in Mikindani Bay was at the small peninsular fishing village, Pemba. The Southern shoreline, sheltered by such a narrow channel that the harbour could almost be described as a lagoon, provided an ideal location for urban expansion as the population grew. These early communities were dependent upon fishing and subsistence agriculture. As the Swahili Coast developed, localised trade followed, based around natural products such as ivory, animal skins and tortoise shells.

A number of Bantu tribes made up Mikindani's population, including the Mahuta from the lower Ruvuma valley, the Makonde from a high inland plateau and small groups of the Yao and Makua tribes among others. The name of the town is believed to have been derived from 'Makinda', a type of small palm tree, although some have suggested that it originates from the tribal name Makonde.

From around the 8th or 9th Century AD the Swahili Coast experienced the expanding influence of the Islamic World. Shirazi Arabs from Persia travelled southwards from the Arabian Gulf, some of them as refugees fleeing persecution in their homeland, and settled in the coastal towns of what is now Tanzania. This influx coincided with the growth of Indian Ocean trade and was followed by a second major wave of immigration, this time from the Indian Subcontinent.

However, it was not until the 18th Century that Mikindani rose to prominence and became a hub of trading activity in the area, in particular for slaves and ivory. Advancements were also taking place in agriculture and industry as a variety of new crops such as millet, maize, sesame and rice were cultivated and the town became the regional shipbuilding capital. Gum copal, orchilla weed and rubber were also traded extensively and Mikindani's population increased in tandem with the economic growth, with ever greater numbers of Arabs, Banyan and Hindi settling in the area.

It was during this period that the first Europeans visited Mikindani. French ships passed through in 1787 seeking slave labour to work on the island plantations of Mauritius and Reunion, with the British Navy soon following. The Sultan of Oman, Seyyid Said, relocated his court from Muscat to Zanzibar in 1832 and actively encouraged his people to settle along the Swahili Coast and develop an infrastructure capable of exploiting the region's natural resources. In terms of prosperity the town was entering what could be described as its golden age, but little of the wealth created had helped the African Swahili community.

Following the Berlin conference of 1884, which precipitated the European colonisation of Africa, the territory of Tanganyika was allocated to Germany. Seeking an immediate economic output from their new colony, the German administration made efforts to increase the scale of local industries, in particular the production of rubber, coconuts and sisal. The regional Governor, Damquat, oversaw the construction of the Boma, a new fort and administrative headquarters, as well as building and renovating the town's Slave Market and Customs House (which is also believed to have served as a slave prison).

An inscription in German above the entrance to the Boma marks the year of its construction.

During the First World War, the German colonial government ceded control of the town to British rule under mandate from the League of Nations. Only a few shots were fired as the Customs House was shelled from the outer bay. However, the ease with which the Royal Navy took Mikindani was by no means indicative of the East Africa conflict in general. In a protracted game of 'cat and mouse', the German General, Paul Emil Von Lettow Vorbeck, fought a brilliant campaign of guerrilla warfare against superior British forces. Such was the esteem in which he was held by his enemies that when, in later life, he was found to be living in destitute poverty, it was arranged for the British Government to pay him a small pension for the remainder of his days.

Following the Second World War, in which Tanganyika saw little conflict, the British administration sought to implement an agricultural plan that would alleviate the shortage of margarine in the British Isles and provide a boost to the output of local trade. Vast tracts of land were set aside (20,000 hectares were initially allocated, but this was soon increased to several million) and a railway constructed from Mikindani to Nachingwea in what became known, notoriously, as the Groundnut Scheme. The project was poorly planned and implemented. Drought, disease and less than ideal growing conditions conspired to render the scheme a failure, and it was abandoned in 1951.

During this period of high hopes and aspirations the regional capital was moved from Mikindani to Mtwara. The new town, which at that point was little more than a cluster of nearby villages, lay 15km to the South and was home to a deep-water harbour more able to accommodate the drafts of larger ships than the shallow channel of Mikindani bay. As quickly as the large, sprawling city of Mtwara grew, Mikindani fell back from prominence and the hum and bustle of commerce and industry departed. It became a quieter, more placid backwater, with only the remnants of once grand buildings revealing a more prosperous past.

The Boma and the Bank House

The Boma, renovated as a not-for-profit, community hotel by the UK charity Trade Aid, overlooks Mikindani Bay. The building in the foreground formerly served as the town's one and only bank.

Above: The Boma was built in 1895 under the supervision of the German colonial governor, Damquat.

Left: The Boma prior to its renovation by Trade Aid in 1997-2000.

Above: The picturesque conference room of the Old Boma Hotel has a majestic view of the bay.

Top Right: The Aga-Khan building is typical of the two-storey buildings in Mikindani's old town. It is currently used as an Islamic school.

Bottom Right: The old slave market. The building's archways, previously open, were filled in during renovation.

The Shia Ithnasheri Mosque

The Hindu Temple

In the Zanzibari style, many old houses in Mikindani have hand-carved wooden doors and door frames.

Coral rocks, or 'rag', are traditionally used as a building material on the Swahili Coast.

Once the largest building in Mikindani, the customs house and prison today lies in ruin.

DAVID LIVINGSTONE

Historically, one of Mikindani's most famous visitors was the Victorian missionary explorer David Livingstone. The Scotsman was already well-known in 19th Century Britain for his travels in Southern Africa and for his attempts to expose and eliminate the horrors of the slave trade through the influence of Christianity and legitimate enterprise.

He arrived in Mikindani from Zanzibar in the spring of 1866 leading a Royal Geographic Society expedition that sought to find the source of the Nile, one of the pre-eminent unsolved mysteries of the time. In his journal, Livingstone remarked that Mikindani had "one of the finest natural harbours on the coast".

The expedition of 1866 proved to be his last journey. After leaving Mikindani, he lost contact completely with the outside world for six years and was plagued by illness for the remainder of his life. During this time he became increasingly determined to see an end to the slavery that he had witnessed and abhorred. In a letter to the editor of the New York Herald he wrote that "if my disclosures regarding the terrible Ujijian slavery should lead to the suppression of the East Coast slave trade, I shall regard that as a greater matter by far than the discovery of all the Nile sources together." The Herald sent the journalist Henry Morton Stanley to find Livingstone in 1869. Their encounter famously took place on the shores of Lake Tanganyika on 10th November 1871, with Stanley greeting the beleaguered explorer with the words "Dr. Livingstone, I presume?"

Despite Stanley's advice that he return to the coast to recuperate and allow time for his health to return, Livingstone determined to continue with his mission. It was not to be. He died on 1st May 1873 in Ilala (a village that now lies in the country of Zambia). His loyal attendants, David Chuma and Abdullah Susi, buried his heart under a tree near to where he died before carrying his embalmed body more than a thousand miles back to the coast and the town of Bagamoyo, where it was returned to London for burial in Westminster Abbey.

Livingstone's legacy inspired abolitionists of the slave trade and he achieved a posthumous level of fame and respect far beyond that which he received during his life. Newspaper stories depicting a man fighting the evil of slavery in the dark continent, obstinately forging on with his mission against all odds and in ill health had struck a chord within Victorian society. His name was henceforth inextricably linked with Africa and with a reputation for humility and dignity that few of his peers shared.

In June 1873 the British Government pressurised the Sultan of Zanzibar into outlawing slavery, which for centuries had ravaged East Africa and devastated whole communities both on the coast and inland. Livingstone's expeditions allowed large swathes of territory in Africa to be mapped and one of the ramifications of his proponency for trade was, arguably, to hasten the establishment of colonial rule. However, his ethical approach to exploration challenged the status quo that imperial countries had a divine right to rule their colonies. He was a strong advocate for the education of indigenous peoples and foresaw the moral pitfalls of colonialism.

In Mikindani today, a plaque commemorates his visit to the town and marks the house in which he was believed to have stayed.

Mnazi Bay, Ruvura Peninsula

This beautiful beach is part of the Mnazi Bay marine reserve and is close to a large, sprawling village called Msimbati. There are miles of white sand and coral reefs close to the shore that teem with an abudance of marine life. Just away from the beach is the ruined house of an eccentric British civil servant who used to live in Tanzania, Latham Leslie Moore. In 1959, he attempted to claim independence from the then colony of Tanganyika and establish Msimbati as a sultanate, for which he even designed a flag. The secession was repressed and he was deported in 1967.

Selling Fish in the Twilight

A dugout canoe reaches the shore at sunset and the fishermen set about sorting their catch and agreeing prices with the middlemen.

The Boat Yard at Mirumba

A group of fishermen head out in the morning mist to check their nets. The building in the background is Mikindani's boat yard.

Dhow on the Bay

Each day it's possible to see dhows crossing between Pemba and Mikindani, their design unchanged after hundreds of years. Their silence and grace are striking when juxtaposed against the noisy, polluting motorised vehicles of the land. Sailing with the fishermen is a unique experience; watch as the triangular sails fill with wind and strain billowing at the mast, the timbers creak and thin streams of iridescent water spread out in the gently heaving wake of the dhow as it glides across the bay.

Baobab Tree

One of the most distinctive trees in East Africa, the baobab tree (Adansonia digitata) is known as the tree of life. For most of the year, the tree is leafless, and looks very much like it has its roots sticking in the air.

Mikindani Harbour

This vista was photograhed from the Livingstone room at the Old Boma in Mikindani. Mikindani Bay was described by the missionary explorer David Livingstone as one of the most perfect natural harbours on the Swahili coastline. The bay is shaped like a spade and the narrow channel at its head keeps the water within relatively calm and sheltered. The left peninsula in this picture is home to a small fishing village called Pemba and the right one is known as Litingi peninsula. Toward the shore you can see fishermen putting out their nets for the day.

Storm on the Horizon

Taken on the outskirts of Mikindani, this image of an electrical thunderstorm expresses one of the extremes of the equatorial monsoon climate. This picture was taken in February during the rainy season; after some 20 minutes of downpour the rain stopped, the clouds broke and a vivid sunset seemed to change the very colour of the air to a deep orange.

Sunset at Yatch

The jetty at the Mikindani Yacht Club, known by the locals as 'Yatch'. The club does not see many yachts, but comprises of a bar and jetty and has been built in Mitengo, one of the quieter, more secluded corners of the bay.

MIKINDANI IN MONOCHROME

Charcoal Cyclists

These men are transporting sackloads of charcoal from Mikindani to the regional capital, Mtwara. They cycle 20km in the mid-day sun with heavy loads bound on Chinese-made 'Phoenix' bicycles. Due to the exploitation of forests for timber export, firewood and charcoal production, deforestation is one of the foremost environmental problems facing Tanzania.

Monsoon Downpour - the long rains hit Mikindani eroding roads, paths and the foundations of buildings. The landscape changes vividly between the dry and rainy seasons.

THE WITCHDOCTOR AND THE CHICKEN

The largest hill in the vicinity of Mikindani Bay is called Mjoho. It was renamed by the Germans in colonial times as Bismarck Hill and, according to old admiralty charts, was used as a reference point for boats navigating the Southern coastline while sailing to and from Mikindani. At the top of the hill is a baobab tree, which the locals call *Mbuyu wa Fedha* (the money tree).

Legend has it that the colonial German forces buried gold at the foot of the tree before fleeing the British Navy and retreating from Mikindani during the Great War. The Royal Navy consolidated its control of the Tanganyikan coastline in 1916 and destroyed Mikindani's Customs House and jail, shelling it from the outer bay on 13th September that year. The hidden German gold has remained a local myth ever since. People often talk about it but few, to my knowledge, have ever tried to find it.

One day in 2000, while walking up the hill, I met an old man with a satchel over his shoulder and a chicken under his arm. He professed to be a witchdoctor and was, he claimed, intent on searching for the hidden German gold. Intrigued, I asked him how he planned on finding it. Did he have an old treasure map where 'x' marked the spot, or a metal detector perhaps?

"No, no. I have a special chicken. A magic one." he said, glowing with pride.

I asked him to elaborate.

"She can show me the location of the treasure. I put her down and where she goes to peck on the ground is where I dig. She is very clever and knows exactly where to go."

To my eyes, it seemed that when he released the startled avian it behaved exactly as any chicken would. It paused and then pranced around, clucking nervously. It raked the ground, pecking aimlessly, hoping to uncover a morsel of food from the detritus. The witchdoctor, however, appeared to have unshakeable confidence in his bird.

I returned to the Mbuyu wa Fedha several weeks later, hoping to climb the baobab and photograph Mikindani Bay as the sun was setting. To my astonishment, there was a hole more than 12 feet deep and 15 feet wide. The amount of earth removed was staggering, it was as though a JCB had been at work. A whole side of the baobab's root structure had been exposed and, as a result of the unearthing, the old tree now listed heavily to one side. The witchdoctor, his tools and his chicken were nowhere to be seen.

I have not seen the old man since that day on the hill. I often wonder if he grew disenchanted with the treasure hunt or lost faith in his chicken. Surely not. Perhaps he has gone to another town or village and is searching afresh for abandoned wealth. Then a thought crosses my mind and brings a smile to my face. What if he was right after all? Perhaps he is now moored in a luxury yacht in the harbour of Dubai or Monte Carlo. Or perhaps this very evening he will be playing the roulette tables of Las Vegas, his magic chicken living alongside him in a lifestyle of royalty.

MIKINDANI IN MONOCHROME

Storm Clouds on Rondo Plateau

BEHIND THE CAMERA

THE PHOTOGRAPHS

In developing this book, I have tried to include a selection of images that might reveal the essence of what makes Mikindani a special place. Inspiration is never far away in Tanzania. Such a beautiful landscape is naturally photogenic and the diverse environment draws you into taking pictures, whether you own a pin-hole camera or a state of the art SLR.

Without doubt, the children in Mikindani are the stars of the book. As time passed they gradually became used to living in the vicinity of someone who kept pointing little black boxes made of plastic and glass at them. Gradually their abject terror at the appearance of a six-foot five mzungu (white man) receded and instead of screaming and running away they started to grin, pose and crouch in martial-arts positions every time they caught a glimpse of my camera, shouting *"piga picha!"*

THE EQUIPMENT

Most images in this book were captured on film. I have always used Fuji film for colour photography and in particular Velvia for its fine grain and intense colour saturation. The colourful clothes, exotic tree blossoms, the clear blue of the Indian Ocean and the blazing red of an African sunset are rendered so vividly by Velvia that it quickly became my film of choice.

The black and white images were taken on Ilford films, usually FP4 Plus and on occasion HP5. When I first discovered black and white photography I found that the tones, textures and contrasts in the Mikindani landscape were brilliantly captured in monochrome. More recently I have turned to the challenging medium of infrared photography using Kodak HIE and Rollei films. All of the 35mm images in the book were obtained using a Minolta Dynax 9 SLR with wide-angle and telephoto zoom lenses.

My digital setup currently consists of a Nikon D200 with Nikkor lenses: 17-55mm and 70-200mm zoom lenses and a 105mm macro lens. RAW files are recorded on Sandisk Extreme IV memory cards and optimised using Adobe Lightroom.

The third photographic system I use in Mikindani is based around the Mamiya 6 medium format camera, a manual rangefinder which yields superb, high-quality negatives and transparencies. As with my Minolta the main films used are Velvia and Ilford FP4 Plus. Nikon scanners were used to digitise the transparencies and negatives with minimal finishing in Adobe Photoshop to remove dust spots and artefacts resulting from the scanning process.

In the field I use polarising and neutral density filters, and a Manfrotto carbon fibre tripod that provides an acceptable compromise between stability and minimal weight – a key consideration when taking this equipment on long walks under the African sun. Thanks must go to my co-volunteers in Trade Aid and the select group of local children in Mikindani who often acted as enthusiastic assistants, running around with camera bags and tripods at dusk trying to find the right spot for all those sunset shots!

ACKNOWLEDGEMENTS

There are a great number of people without whose support, inspiration and companionship this book would never have been published.

Firstly I would like to thank Brian Currie. His drive and dedication in creating and overseeing the charity Trade Aid have made a great deal of difference to my life and those of many others. Since its inception, the charity has provided stable employment for around forty members of the local community, improving living standards for them and their dependents and family members. The project has also enabled more than thirty gap year students and a large number of experienced volunteers from the UK to work in one of Tanzania's poorest regions.

Many thanks must go to the staff and managers in Trade Aid who I have worked with over the years, in particular: Jacob Amuli, Simon Waane, Dennis Massoi, Arthur Poulton, Sherie Williams-Ellen, Andy Partridge, David Chivers, Ian Smith, Sandra Francis-Love, Jean Milnes, Sue Button, Yvonne Munnichs, Donna Wright, Katy Davies, David Wedick, Kynan Buckingham and Kate Methley. Volunteers who kept me out of (and occasionally got me into) trouble include Dan Cherry, Nick Andrews, Matt Maddocks, George Barrett, Emily Jackson, Tim Dench, Tom Herbert, Becky Stickland and Tim Crouch.

The staff at the Old Boma have always been a big part of my life in Mikindani. I'd like to thank all of my friends there, especially Maggie and Emma Mwambe, Vicky Millanzi, Esther Thomas, Joyce Hittu, Dickson Kamanga, Chris Liundi, Hamisi Mchopa, Shaibu Kajonjo, Ahmadi Abdallah, Fatuma Ali, Asha Salum, Bimkubwa Hassani, Mohamed Mzanda, Sarah Mukhsin, Hadija Mlaponi, Mohamed Ahmed, Asha Saidi, Ajuae Issa and the legendary Salum Mtipa. My thoughts and thanks also lie with friends no longer with us: Janet Green, Mecline Mwita and Rukia Hamisi.

I am indebted to Sofia Cababie for her expertise and dedication towards the design and layout of this book. I am also extremely grateful to Lucy-Michael Sutton and Matt Wood for their support, input and patience in reviewing my images and iterations of the written chapters. I would like to show my appreciation to Barry Codrington, Jane Langford and Paul Hennessy for their constructive feedback and incisive suggestions whilst proof-reading my drafts. I'm also grateful to my brother Ben for his efforts on the website. Finally, I am indebted to my parents for their guidance, support and understanding as I drop everything and return to Tanzania each year.

Lastly but most importantly I would like to express my gratitude to my friends and acquaintances in the community of Mikindani. There are many people who have played a part in my life in Tanzania to whom I am very grateful, but unfortunately I do not have the space to mention them all individually (the list would fill the book on its own). However, special thanks must go to the Liloko family, Mohamed Ali Doa, my neighbour Bibi Zaidu, Tumaini Namadengwa, Hadija Ally, Fatuma Mohamedi, Asha Hassani and the irrepressible Ali Mapolulu.